Praise for *Fire*

Twenty-nine poets, all members of the Writers' Group of the Triad, have pooled their considerable talent and creative energy to produce as delightful an anthology as I've had the pleasure to read in quite some time. The book is divided into thematic units, a structure which allows the individual poems in each section to converse, so to speak, with one another, bringing a greater resonance to the whole....

This is poetry that doesn't sacrifice truth to artifice or sense to sensational effects. While striving, as poets always have done, to reach beyond the limitations of ordinary language, these writers never try to seem profound by being obscure. Rather, they give voice to many of the recognizable modalities of our human condition, such as joy in nature, sorrow for irretrievable losses, and plain delight in the small pleasures of everyday life. To open this admirable book is truly to wander into a "gathering of gifted friends," as Diana Engel puts it in her fine introduction, and no poetry lover could hope for more satisfying company.

Mark Smith-Soto, Editor, *International Poetry Review*, and author of three prize-winning poetry chapbooks and two collections, *Our Lives Are Rivers* (University Press of Florida, 2003) and *Any Second Now* (Main Street Rag Publishing Co., 2006). The winner of an NEA fellowship in 2005, he teaches at The University of North Carolina at Greensboro.

The poems in Fire and Chocolate *are offered as sacrament to the seasons of human unfolding that transpire between heaven and earth. Within these pages, one's soul will be led on a sensuous journey from the sweetest sublime through the dark and earthy bittersweet of love and disappointment. Through it all though, the precision with which these poems are crafted will bring delight in the thanksgiving these poems engender and will leave the reader renewed, confirmed and again believing in the power of poetry as prayer.*

Anjail Rashida Ahmad, Director, The Creative Writing Program, North Carolina Agricultural and Technical State University

i

For those of us who have a special affection for Greensboro and the Triad, there's a special joy in retrieving the local images and memories offered up in the Writers' Group of the Triad's poetry anthology Fire and Chocolate: *sweeping the floor of a forest's "dried leaf playhouse, a puff of dust / beneath our sprouting wings" or walking through Battleground Park, where "beneath the pine needles / and red clay soil / rest the bones of soldiers."* Yet these poems also escort us all around the world—from the *"rouge-marked Madrones"* at San Damiano to *"the bloated sun rising and setting / its same steady ordinance"* in Laos and *"the darkening shade / of a frangipani and a flame tree"* in Chad. These well-selected, thoughtfully organized poems ask us to look at the commonplace elements of the world— heat lighting, the *"telegraph-T"* of phone lines, *"crooked old dogs"*—and, by giving them what Wordsworth calls *"a certain colouring of imagination,"* make them seem mysterious and new.

Janice Moore Fuller, author of *Séance and Sex Education*, Writer-in-Residence, Catawba College

The poems in this new anthology open their arms to the reader—they are welcoming as the parks and gardens of Greensboro, yet document a search for solace which remains as unattainable as the moon. Family and solitude, love and loss, sea and soil—" … why is it that things so coarse / must be handled with delicate / maneuvers and drawn-out / patience?" The Writers Group of the Triad brings together in these 130 pages a gathering of flowers, indeed, a blossoming of formal and free verse, haiku and prose poems. These poets have learned how to use the "crazy glue" of words to bind up shattered lives, to comfort and challenge, and to lift the beauties of the world in celebration. I found old friends in this anthology, and welcomed many new ones. A rewarding volume!

Valerie Nieman, author of *Wake Wake Wake* (Press 53, 2006), is a professor at North Carolina Agricultural and Technical State University.

Fire and Chocolate

fire & chocolate

POEMS FROM THE
WRITERS' GROUP OF THE TRIAD

Edited by
Coventry Kessler, Ellen Summers, and Diana Engel

Writers' Group of the Triad
Greensboro, NC

Published by Writers' Group of the Triad
www.TriadWriters.org

Copyright © 2011 by the Contributors

Cover Design © 2011 Imagine! Studios™ LLC
www.artsimagine.com

Cover photo by Caren Masem

Layout and sequencing by Coventry Kessler

For permission to reprint poems that first appeared in publications listed below, we give grateful acknowledgment to those publications' editors.

Fran Ostasiewski, "Playing the Odds," *Frogpond*, Volume 31:2, 2008 and *White Lies: The Red Moon Anthology of English-Language Haiku*, 2009; "harvest moon sliver," *Frogpond*, Volume 34:2, 2011.

Jean Rodenbough, "At San Damiano," *Wild Goose Poetry Review*, August 2010; "The Woods," First Place Award, Burlington Writers Club, 2011.

Anya Russian, "Light," *International Poetry Review*, Spring 2011; "Walking the Line" and "Call to Prayer" (both revised), Nazim Hikmet Poetry Festival (Cary, NC), 2010; "A Visitor," *Pinesong*, North Carolina Poetry Society Awards, 2010.

ISBN: 978-0-9849349-0-4

First Writers' Group of the Triad printing, January 2012

Preface

Dear Reader,

The most memorable poetry is a place where the sensuous springs to life. We find ourselves taking in the sights, sounds, smells, and flavors a poet serves us. As you plumb the riches of this collection, you will find that its title, *Fire and Chocolate*, is apt.

Watch the sudden blaze of light and listen to the echoing thunder: "kettledrums and fire" while the California Zephyr speeds through dark prairies in Judith Behar's poem, "Lightning." Taste the luscious depths of "sixty percent cacao" as you read Barbara Baillet Moran's "How to Eat Chocolate." Wander barefoot over warm cobblestones of Paris with Rhoda Cerny in "I Want to Wear Dresses."

These poems and the many others gathered here sing of the journey we are all taking. Each poet is a wayfarer stopping to recount the light and the dark, the complexity of human relationships, the grandeur and terror of nature, the disappointing brokenness of our human world and how compassion becomes beauty magnified, ironically more intense and cherished in such a context.

Poetry is the genre that races to the heart of its subject in only a few lines, frequently pulling out all the stops—giving us, as readers, musical language, startling imagery, and often meter and rhyme to take us to a place of revelation and surprise. That is the kind of verse you will discover in this anthology.

As you read these poems, you may note some instances of punctuation, spelling, or formatting that are non-standard. One of the joys and challenges of editing poetry is that poets do not always follow the rules. Hopefully, I and my fellow editors caught all the actual errors and any that remain can be chalked up to "poetic license."

I am humbled to participate in the Writers' Group of the Triad Poetry Writers evening critique group, a gathering of gifted friends who teach me about skillful writing as well as about life with the poems that they bring to each meeting. Without the submissions of the twenty-nine WGOT poets whose writing illuminates these pages and their generous participation in the process, there would be no anthology.

Fire and Chocolate is a reality due also to the vision and investment of the WGOT Board of Directors. The board gave this project its beginning and the support needed for its production. Judy Behar, WGOT Publicity Director, has been extremely helpful in scheduling promotional events.

I am particularly grateful to my creative and hard working partners, the editing team: Coventry Kessler and Ellen Summers. Steve Wessells lent an extra set of keen eyes and ears that assisted us in the process of selection. Kristen J. Eckstein's donation of time and talent assured us a fine design for cover and book. And without Rosalyn Marhatta and her marvelous publicity and marketing committee, which includes Jean Rodenbough, Caren Masem, Tony Hardy, and Rhoda Cerny, this collection would not be in the hands of readers within our community.

I also owe a measure of gratitude to the Children's Writers and Memoir Group facilitators: Chris McCarthy, Sandra Redding, and Marie Sechrest, who shared their ideas with us. Many thanks to all who made this anthology possible.

In closing, may you, dear reader, savor the experiences captured in the lines of every poem.

To celebrate the spirit of humanity and nature in vivid verse,

Diana Engel
Facilitator of WGOT's Poetry Writers (evening group)

Contents

LOVE AND LOVE GONE WRONG

AROUND THE WORLD AND HOME

ART, WRITING, AND ALL THAT JAZZ

FIRE AND CHOCOLATE

Lightning

Judith Behar

The California Zephyr connects
Chicago to the coast, speeds
across empty prairies—
night descending
from the dome of sky
through the car's glass dome.

Heat lightning over Iowa
flashes on the horizon, pulses
into blackness, sparks again
over the rocketing train.
A first-time traveler huddles
between the power overhead
and on the tracks, zapped
by the immensity of the land,
the force that plays with kettledrums
and fire as the train clacks out
the miles from home.

Years later she'll remember journeying alone,
the cottonwoods and grasses,
the towns passed through, the yards
with work clothes on the line, children waving,
the chilled air in the observation car,
awe and immensity, lightning blazing in the dark.

How To Eat Chocolate

Barbara Baillet Moran

It is not mere chocolate, as chocolate lovers know.
True lovers love true chocolate,
sixty percent cacao: a dark, murky velvet.
Luscious, bittersweet, and holy mud.

Should the chocolatier choose
to probe mythic depths
and heights,
sample wine-like symphonic notes
and overtones—and this is only
about chocolate, remember—
then, my dears, sugar must go.

Sweetness deceives tender taste buds,
offending their delicate dignity.
Seduced by vile white crystals,
the novice chews the cold chunk,
finds only cloying, puny flavor.
The precious moment squandered.

Poor postulant never knows
the slow warming melt
in the mouth's moist oven
of sixty percent cacao,
the divine swirl, the gentle yielding essence,
a final dark elixir unfolded,
sliding down
at last
into sublime
memory.

NATURAL WORLD

In Wilderness

Stephen G. Wessells

All my past moments sift like dry sand
through my fingers; wind puffs them away
to the high dunes of my history, which swallow
even wary steps. If I dare climb,
I see one sand horizon past another
and there is no end or variation.
On this desert no mercy of rain;
however many tears, no flower blooms.
On this desert, old howls of regret
blow every footprint back into the sand,
choke every pathway out.
Here the cold nights leech all heat of passion
toward the stars that mock unreachably;
from their remote, walled heaven there drifts
a song of light that silences all prayers.
All who walk that desert walk alone.
The adder and the scorpion lie in wait,
coiled in the scraps of shade, eager to strike,
and every camel spits into your eye.
The desert breeds only madmen or saints
(often the same people), and somewhere
(I heard rumored) past all this wind-scoured wilderness,
if I can steel my mind against mirages,
date palms cast their shade upon cool waters.
At that unwalled oasis all may drink
who give up searching and embrace their thirst.
Yet every ocean that refreshed my sight
a lie of heat spread falsely over sand;
every cactus speared me with its thorns
and gave no water. Every cooling drink
sweated away, lost in the parched Ein Gedi
of forgotten dreams and lying promises.

How came I here? Turn these stones into bread.
Unreel the kingless kingdoms of the world,
I will not worship or bow down to them.
Strike off my shackles and I have no home.
I am the storied wanderer. For a song
or tale of far-off lands the villagers
will spread a pallet for me for a night;
I trade my birthright for their bowl of stew.
I learn to love my solitude, I court
a sky soared over by my eyes alone,
I woo my isolation like a bride.

Beneath the vault of these unpeeled heavens
I alone am king, without a rival.
All the dead souls that gave birth to me
fall on their faces. They don't know I hear
their secret snickering, nor that I know
that in a moment I'll be one of them,
pushing the unborn me into his future.
The desert of regrets has no horizon.
All hope withers there, seared by the heat
of failures past. Let go. Sink into sand.
Let every sight of sky be smothered up;
nothing beyond myself shall live—the world
shall be the womb from which shall squeeze
all my stillborn tomorrows.
                              Never mind.
There are dark, swift rivers underground—
if I sink deep enough, I shall fall through
and ride them, amniotic, to the sea.

A Roaring in the Night: April 28, 2011

Susan Dean Wessells

I'm wakened from soft sleep and gentle dreams;
a roaring in the night, like rumbling
of a heavy engine thundering on rails,
wrenches me aware.

Memories of southbound freight go chugging through my mind.
Then, waiting for the call of whistle-sound, what comes to me
is that no locomotive can be heard
from where I rest.
I am now wide awake,

and the menace of the angry storm is clear.
No thunder claps, but one continuous growl,
as though some ravenous prowling beast is near,
now snapping at the heels of reverie,
fangs tearing at the fabric of my fear.

With one last rancorous snarl
the twisting rage departs,
and though the night is quiet once again,
some time will pass before my thundering heart
resumes a restful beat,
and sleep transports me on a milder train.

Cloud

Ellen Summers

A cloud of birds,
ten thousand birds, at first tickling
the earth for seeds,
each an atom
rising gently along with others, others,
a galaxy of brothers
speckling the sky,
flipping clipped wings in beats
ticking, quickening,
lifting
as a mass,
as an audience claps,
as a celebrant prays,
each one flapping its flippers, dapples and
darkens silence
with breath.
Heaving the land, the altar,
upward, they fly, a floating continent,
over the line of folded hills,
beyond planes of sight and sound.
Perhaps they are rising still
beyond the orbit of Earth,
sparks in the calming darkness,
the velvet womb of worlds,
winging, but silently, airlessly
drifting into my dreams
of living forever.

The Moon is the Best Thing on Earth

Catherine Ashley-Nelson

I

Up there it is but a large cold rock
pocked with craters,
its surface cut by rifts,
blotched by shadow "seas."
And moon dust, from what I've seen,
is much like desert dust,
no mirror glint to its whirling.

So I'm amazed each time I see it.

I can't see Arizona,
though the sun still shines upon it
after dark enshrouds this tree-full place.
It is a nice thought, though:
Arizona a ruddy glow,
like a second sunset,
reminding me of those years
of sunsets—all the hues of passion—
of the distance
between us,
much greater than that
between earth and moon.

II

In Arizona I could lie on a cot
under the moon and stars
three hundred and fifty nights a year
and listen to the desert breathe,
the coyote's howl, a scorpion's scraping
stroll across a rock, the moon sometimes
scarcely a nail paring, sometimes
the concave face of a puppet
with pointed chin and hat,
once each month a platinum globe,
a perfect circle
as though cut from white paper

and pasted onto a navy night,
an art project of a schoolgirl
who knows where magic lies,
has found the benevolent god
a reflection of her own bright light.

III
Once in a dusky full-moon rising,
a friend stood on top of a mesa,
positioned just so, head tilted back,
her mouth wide open.
Someone took her picture and
I am jealous still.
It should have been I in that photo,
for all the times
I've swallowed the moon,
made my insides glow.

IV
If you could drive in a tunnel
through the center of the moon,
you could reach the opposite side
in less time than it would take you
to motor from Charlotte to L.A.
If circumnavigating the moon,
you could cover the distance
from New York (as the crow flies)
to the far side of the Aegean Sea,
an exhausting trip perhaps,
but an imaginable journey.

I think of that,
reduce the moon to earthy terms,
in rare moments
when I cannot bear the light
or do not deserve it.

V
If I had created the heavens and earth,
I would have made more moons.

Dragonfly

Diana Engel

in memory of my aunt, Carol McMillan Godel

Iridescent dancer,
lapis lake skimmer,
light's lavish lark

*Four-spotted chaser** of
water's mist from
Alaska to Paraguay,
Idaho to the Caymans

Surface-skirting pond damsel,
darning needle
weaving serpentine patterns
of aquatic illusion

Red-veined darter,
fleet optical flier,
ruby meadow-hawk,
my dreams' sailing bark

* Terms in italics designate species of dragonflies.

Fran Ostasiewski

harvest moon sliver
the pond no longer reflects
her darkness

Winter Marsh

Janice L. Sullivan

Close
to the wetlands
a jogger
watches
a white egret,
waits for her
to pluck
tiny krill
and fish
from the bog.
The jogger
understands
this egret
is patient
as an old man
fishing
from
a wooden dock.

Mountain Waterfall

Caren Masem

Almost beyond reach
pied blue streams
of waters fall
below the bark
of Douglas firs
and fuzzy emerald
rocks along the trail.
Its crashing, splashing
voice calls me to climb
towards its origin,
a high country lake.

I tried so many times
to see that cascade
held in place by earth,
the eternal pull of belief.
Though time takes
all it ever wants, I fight.
I will own the silky cool
before it will be night.

Bindings for the Sea

Stephanie McManus

This sisal rope binding
is itchy and coarse,
untangling
strand by strand;
fingers pick and pull
burning raw.
I know this
rope must be not
snapped
but delicately unraveled . . .

(. . . why is it that things so coarse
must be handled with delicate
maneuvers and drawn-out
patience?)

The multiple demands
by others and self
bind to us tighter and tighter
infiltrating gears and mechanisms
of the brain that control basic functions
like Breath
and
Blink,
until shimmering,
we are pulsating energy potentials
threatening to explode
all over a simple
"Hello."

A screaming banshee goddess
taking up issue with this
invasion of "must-be-dones"
and plans within plans,
swinging to and fro on
a rickety wooden swing ten feet
off the ground
(good balance is necessary,
and it *is* such good fun)—
this goddess does not do
compromise for
multiple tunes . . . she just sings,
and when roped into another song,
as this song is, we title it:

"Discord" or "Bound."

But I, like a caterpillar
underside a leaf,
for what reasons would I choose
to bear such heavy grief?

Let's go back to the sea,
throw our bindings overboard,
make them walk the plank
even, laughing loud and lovely,
and it will be sunny and the wind
will blow strong, a god's hug;
and in this space
of memory. . .
we'll be unfettered by it all,
simply.

The Woods

Jean Rodenbough

I'd not have come here
if not for dogs. First
the big black one and then
the little hunter; their noses
take us along deer paths,
over stumblesome roots
of trees—ah, the trees—
   the great one, smooth-barked,
   crippled in rough branches,
   wind-broken, enduring—
   the lesser trees give space
   to age and strength.

Deer tracks, 'coon scat,
abandoned squirrel digs;
overhead, crows convene—
below, the dogs trail mystery
   while I am lost
   beneath the tree
   whose exposed roots, like dragon-toes,
   stretch toward . . . something.

Dizzy from looking up and up its limbs,
I touch this trunk to steady myself;
its life, electric to my hands,
centers me here. I am not lost.
Here. Beneath
one gray-twigged branch,
one green leaf.

Yard in Late Winter

Lynne Martin Bowman

The low-slung yellow moon blurs and stars dim
in the rising haze of late winter warming; the budding
trees begin to block the sky too early, their green
at night the sweet sick scent of spring becoming.

The moon seems a far-flung bone; our dog
now chasing the raccoon might end up finding it
tucked deep and out of air, with his galloping, his circling,
his dead-on nose for things we cannot see.

The moon's no better than a bone to him, or less—
too far, too dry, too cold, too empty of flesh and blood,
no flakes of skin that make the scent, the tiny trails
of what is breathing, was breathing, the sort of speech
heard only by what might take the breath away.

Entering Trees

Diana Engel

A wind-weaving voice calls
through sky-vaulted corridors of pines
from the far side of this forested world.
Bullfrogs cease their rhythmic croaking
to listen.
Sunlight strikes the face of a deer
moving in the brake of trees.

A doe,
liquid eyes like my daughter's,
speaks nature's mystery with her gaze
startling as a crow's sudden caw,
sends my mind plunging
well-deep into these woods
dropping a bucket through time.

I see Ethiopia's thorny myrrh,
its ancient bark severed by Theias' arrow,*
bleed resin tears:
the holy oil of the Jews,
drink refused by dying Christ,
sweet perfume for lovers' beds.

In British Gaul
against trunks of weeping willows
druid priests and priestesses lean
waiting for the eloquence
of the grove to inhabit them
the way birds nest in branches.

And somewhere in Camelot
a towering oak keeps watch
for young King Arthur
transformed into a merlin
to finish his circling and seek her shade.

Trees,
soul water of reflection
and creation's treasure chest,
silently observe the centuries unfold:
broadleafed sycamores mark soldiers sacrificed
on war's battlefields.
Mississippi gallows trees whisper the names of hatred's victims.

My journey ends
in a canopy of childhood hickories
where I find my mother
with hammer in hand.
She nails a pale pine rail
into the quadrangle,
finishing the family tree house
as a wren begins to sing.

* Greek myth: In the dark of night, Theias, King of Syria, is deceived
by his daughter Myrrha into sleeping with her. Once he realizes
what has happened, he chases after her. As he shoots an arrow
toward her, she becomes a myrrh tree and Adonis is born.

Autumn's Wooing

Stephen G. Wessells

The lying and adulterous Autumn light
spills its gold upon the leaves, then leaves;
so every glory tarnishes its bright
beginning, and its progeny bereaves;
a story no less sad for being old
as dust, which our proud bodies shall become.
Considering how often it is told,
why am I not despairing? I am numb.
Let beauty still deceive, entice, beguile
until we're lost and hopelessly entranced;
at least we had her for a little while.
She left at dawn, but in the night we danced;
a brief flirtation in this life, but we
plan to elope into eternity.

Arboreal Aria

Gail Barger

It stood near the sidewalk,
giant arms stretched outward,
sylvan hair twisted
dramatically to one side,
face contorted by a gaping,
gnarled mouth.

At first I thought
the tree a monster,
howling,
long, low, and deep.
A wail originating from
its very roots
expelled into the universe
with heart-wrenching intensity.
A release of such
turbulent magnificence
summons angels, devils,
shatters hearts,
cracks the sky.
Something beyond
human ears thundered
through my senses.
An arboreal aria,
operatic, transcendent, ancient.
I, the only human recipient.

Euphoric Euphorbia

Rhoda Cerny

Euphorbia lactea,
White Ghost,
milky cactus phantom.

Shadow-side,
black blood-tinged fangs
puncture your bone-white arms.
Hypnotizing travelers,
you are an ancient road sign mirage,
leading towards a ghastly dead-end.
Pallid skeletal pointer to Tombstone,
silver ghost towns,
wherever there is a past.
Whispering snowy-cloud kachina,
ethereal ivory shaman
harboring the vanishing ones.
Alabaster desert death tree,
guardian of marble orchards.

Illuminated,
your Far Eastern charm frolics,
lifting souls.
Euphoric euphorbia,
your pearly body is a face
of age-old wisdom,
animated and still.
Your Buddha bulbs smile
at local greenhouse chatter,
an ivory joke with no punchline,
Mahakashyapa's laugh
resonant through time.

Haunting happy moon,
only a specter
of your dazzling sun sister *Ruby*.
Her green is that of youth;
you are chalky,
of the grave.
While she hotly preens,
soaking in the glory of the day,
you shimmer in silvery suchness—
a cool Zen reminder
that things are as they should be.

Watching the Eclipse with Her Cat

Catherine Ashley-Nelson

His coat the color of starless night,
His eyes green-gold moons,
Eclipsed at centers by gloss-black ovals
The size of planets,
He questions, again, his person.

She clasps him tightly in her arms,
Kisses his nose,
Takes him into the dusk
Where the sky is a smoke-blue slate.
She babbles as always:
"The sun, my darling, the earth, the moon
Are all aligned tonight."

Over her shoulder he watches
The blinded eye in the sky,
The color of rust.

She watches him watch,
Her joy receding with the darkness—

For in the returning light, she sees,
As through the wrong end of a telescope,
Through this prism of love,
Beyond this prison of love,
Encrypted behind his own moons,
A knowledge of eclipses
Too vast to fathom
With the naked human eye.

Fire and Chocolate

Cats

Judith Behar

pretend to domesticity
but form their own society
with strict formalities
their servants only guess

identify their territories
set up their private boundaries
by rubbing on upholsteries
and creating mess

but sometimes when they cuddle up
their sweetness seems to bubble up
their purring seems to double up
then we know happiness

The Fawn and the Mole

Gail Barger

You inched forward
on hands and knees
for a closer look
at the terrified fawn
curled under the back deck.
Its eyes squinted
in pain or fear.

Kneeling and peering
into the heat duct,
I saw a small fat mole
stuck in a crack,
afraid, quivering,
trying to squirm
its way free.

The fawn was revealed:
a long forgotten
roll of insulation.
Under flashlight beam
the plump mole,
a piece of loose duct tape
flapping in the breeze.

You and I
illusions, too.
Imaginations ablaze,
our possibilities
illuminated and vanished.
Fog burning off the sea.

Marimbondo

Rhoda Cerny

My mind squirms
in the web of the world,
wrapping,
hopelessly tied
to frothing Diabolo strings
vibrating between my ears,
spinning from the black widow
I cannot see.

Frozen by sticky tendrils,
I silently suffer the sinews of another's wiry plan.

I will pretend
the gossamer is calm;
numb my perception,
rock gently
on the arachnid hammock,
swatting the negative thoughts
which bring on the Queen's army—
small eight-legged warnings
that the Big Black Death is watching,
keeping count of every slippery stumble
in her hourglass.

Protect me,
Marimbondo—
golden spider wasp.
Paralyze her
and lay your golden eggs in her belly,
bury her with the soil of life.
Only then,
when your giant larva emerges to devour her,
will my frightened soul rest in my own cocoon.

Some Place

Stephanie McManus

Collapsing
in the grass
I am a
galaxy
      filament
             unraveling;
here, orchids rain—
a thought hiccup
from that state of
somnolence.

Reclining upon
the dendrobium's jaw,
I am an alien creature
rising up and out
into outer space;
we are spinning,
swinging each leg
at the speed of light
through dark matter.
I am the flower propeller,
swinging in anti-gravity
on my orchid.

Back on earth
the sun is setting
after a long day
and "some place" is
this space not here
not anywhere but
in a flicker—
serenity is a humming hush
in the cacophony
of all of these "musts."

Fire and Chocolate

After Reading Wendell Berry's "The Peace of Wild Things"

Judith Behar

How orderly we wish
the world: The sun
to rise and set, the moon
to wax and wane,
warm winds and crocuses
to follow winter storms,
summer's sweaty days give way
to autumn shine—yet
everywhere earth quakes,
erupts in fire and slag
while winds grow fierce,
drought withers crops,
floods drown whole towns
in mud, dams break, roads crumble,
fog shrouds survivors' minds
and chills their hearts.

Silently the wild things
disappear: the frogs,
the bees, the fireflies.
Cicadas' hum
and crickets' song diminish.
Clams, fish, and pelicans
are bathed in oil, sludge
darkens a marsh
where alligators loll. For clam diggers,
fishermen, watchers of birds and men,
auguries of death disrupt
the peace that heals.

Transcend Dance

Stephen G. Wessells

One morning the wind yanked me out of myself
and swept me away to a land of music and moonlight.
Gypsies cast bones on the grass and read
the fortunes of the dying in the dead.
Wolves in the distance sang the cantatas of wildness.
Where was I dancing? Threading the purple branches
of winter-worn maples and oaks, pursuing
the white moths of wisdom, flakes of moonlight
that froze on their fall through the chilling
sublunary regions, cutting the mocking spirits
who circle the earth in search of
lost deeds to redeem.
                              Earth is the shadowed planet
blighted with life, say the stars,
who have cast from their fire
every nature more dense than their own.
But here, in the humble courtesy of living,
we allow other beings into our breath.
Come, toads and tarantulas, cockroaches,
ticks and mosquitoes, drinkers of blood,
you are here for a reason. Hunters and prey
scorn the pride of the vaulting heavens. In shadow,
their shelter, they stalk and deceive in the night
that embraces and dances with all, with me—
arms wide to them all, I drink the
embrace of the moonlight, just before dawn.

LOVE AND LOVE GONE WRONG

If You Were Mine to Love

Coventry Kessler

If you were mine to love,
I'd paint your toenails red,
Twine ivy through your hair,
Spill wine from the alabaster cup
To drink from your wine-sweet skin.

Run screaming with the maenads,
Leap naked through the groves,
And dance thanks to Dionysius
For the gift of wild-heart love.

I Can't Come Home Today

Coventry Kessler

An explanation to husbands when their wives get that faraway look...

I can't come home today.
Today I am out in the woods with Love
Getting my ringlets curled.

Tomorrow I'll be back
To wash the cups
And stir the stew
And mind the kids
And pay the bills
And pay my attention to you.

But not until tomorrow—
For today I am out in the woods with Love
Getting my ringlets curled.

Fire and Chocolate

I Want to Wear Dresses

Rhoda Cerny

I want to wear dresses:
short, thin, summery, French.
The kind to fling across a chair
on a hot day
before hopping into
a smooth cool bed
with a warm hairy French man.

So wear one,
the feminists
and the men say,
without romance.

But I cannot wear one
the way it is meant to be felt.
My calves are not the shapely bronze
of a fit French woman.
Rather, ashamed like palm-heart blocks,
white, frond-bald
behind the dark curtains
of a long skirt.

Who cares, just wear what you like,
say the feminists
and the men,
without romance.

They fail to understand
the feeling I desire,
the dream of light cloth
against my chipper silky thighs.

I imagine my own as they could be—
springing with ease
above warm bare feet
on dusty cobblestones.
Smiling to myself,
turning heads
in France.

Go ahead,
be proud of your womanly legs;
don't compare yourself
unrealistically to others,
they say.
Plenty of French women
have big thighs
and are beautiful.
Beauty is an attitude.
Men like full figures…
You should be grateful.

Goat cheese.

They fail to understand
the importance of the angle
of my small supple knees
winking from under a bistro table
at handsome passers-by,
inviting them for a milky coffee
on a stifling day
in Paris.

Nor the pleasure of
feeling small, flighty,
radiant, innocent,
carefree.

So I cannot do as they say.
I am not a French woman
and my legs are not thin.
I will wear dresses
but with a few extra inches
to cover the palm-hearts,
safely hiding my faults
and my fantasies,
diluting the romance,
ignoring the logic
of the feminists and men.

Light

Anya Russian

Between the draped curtains
a splinter of light traces
the day's casual invitation,
a door slightly left ajar.
Clasped in the sheet's folds
the body is a mysterious architecture—
a still, unfaltering prayer,
a locket broken by announcement.
I give you my knee
softly raised like a dune,
a fist tucked underneath my chin,
the shallow dip between my legs.
I offer these minor proportions
these arms, these limbs
these teeth,
these dreams
made acute
in their absence.
Please, if you will
diagnose the shade
in this room,
the countenance of the shoes
drying in the corner,
the contented spoon
propped in a dirty glass.
Swallow this white continent
that drifts through
the map of hours
collecting the scrap pieces
of motions that fall,
neglected by time—
you who perform minor surgeries
on the edge of my shoulder,
who divide into north and south
my relinquished territory;

you who measure with ruler
the anxious perimeters
of an unknown reach,
who inquire knowingly
across my sculpture
in bas relief—you,
a welcome aside
like the tilt of a head,
an accidental voyage,
the arched lips of a vase.
You who've mastered
the art of spareness
cast me your reign,
your plume,
your horn,
your pharaoh's warning
    grace
strained from its source.

Lovelight

Stephen G. Wessells

As if the stars had left the skies
to sport like dolphins in your eyes,
something celestial in them rides
my rocky shores like ocean tides;

then let your love's reflected light
kindle with tears my starless night,
and in their welling seas immerse
a new-created universe.

Memory Still

Stephanie McManus

I need photographs of you to remember
the way you smiled at me,
moments that cannot be re-
drawn with crayons
or pounded into the present
with frustrated shrieks.

I have a string.
It is a thread of grey,
long and trailing behind over
the horizon; I am walking
on a highway back
somewhere—

where has that place gone?

If I follow the thread back,
will I find you there?

I don't really need the photographs
to remember; it is that I
wish to flesh out memory until
you are standing before me—

a reflection of who I am
and so spectacularly,
who you are

and tip-toe up to kiss you
gently, breathing life
that was gone
into your eyes

to see you smile.

Afternoon in Eden

Julius Howell

Early afternoon, I awake to your presence—
your smile—your kiss—your fragrance.

Eyes open hazily.
Arms, looping lazily,
        making daisy chains.

Lips curl with love, unspoken.
Dreams lift like vapors, rising.

Pools of sweat echo waterfalls.
Crashing waves still reverberate in hollow halls,
        trapping tender moans of yesterday.

Downcast eyes catch glimpses of Eden.
Tongues sting of bittersweetness,
and the air reeks of half-eaten fruit.

Today is due tomorrow.
Without pockets, we quake.

What have we done?

To Calm the Sea

Robin E. Kelly

I chart a boat to sail away upon the open sea. The wind, the froth,
the foam and spray—none change the soul in me.

I ride a wave, care for it not, and never give ye sway. The wind, the
waves, the countless days—they matter in no way.

Except for her, for when she speaks, tsunami moves upon the deep.
My ship pulls into bay to seek respite from the fray.

The winds and waves of torrent calm. Her lovely wake, it sets me
down to rest at last before her as she sits to speak.

She calms the sea and fight in me; I do not know just how. I cannot
fight it though I try—she brings me to the bow.

She steps off board and leaves me be, and I return to blustery me. I
cannot wait till port I make with the reins for her to take and let her
calm the sea.

Love and Be Silent

Ellen Summers

The feeling gropes for words
and is no longer what it is.
The lover speaks, and love
slips out the door unnoticed,
a guest no longer welcome for herself
but for her name upon the list.

Love and be silent.
Work all night long:
word-weaving done in daylight
to cover and belie, unravel.
Pray and weep in darkness,
build and feather no nest,
and you will know what love is.

Fire and Chocolate

Anniversary

A. C. Hardy

Today, one year later,
I think of the day you said
that things had changed.
I think of the way you spoke,
how sunlight drifted
across your face.
Particles of the air
moved to your will,
focused, and hurled me
down to the earth.

And today
I think of all the ways
that we betrayed
one another . . .
You may have known
(having that
strange intuition
denied to men)
that I was
already gone.

The Lie

Jane Gibson Brown

In the Greek
a lie is something
from which one can
learn nothing.
So when I tell you
where I have been
and what I have done,
you won't know exactly
who and what and when
I took flight to bend
my ordinary day
or went down the alleys
to reach passion fruit streets
or did a thing so wicked
that I need the lie
for you and for me.
A lie may make you dumb
but it doesn't make me free.

Tide Song

Rosalyn Marhatta

There is no mooring
to anchor the heart
when clouds toss boats
in storms of silver ice.

Filaments attach
themselves in lovers' hearts
to push and pull
them between tides of frost
and fire.

You half float in my eyes
as I sip margaritas
on shore.
You sit there in your captain's chair
sailing your life away from mine.

Still, attachment cannot be cut
while sails
half filled with promises
fly overhead.

For Public Consumption

Nancy Jackson

You would do well, my friend, to start praying for the poor sot who attempts to capture my attention.

That he brings with him a 20-mule team to drag my heart from where it is already mired in love.

That his armor is strong and his skin thick to withstand the axe balanced in my hand and the daggers poised on my lips, ready to flay and dismember him for the crime of being less than you.

That his mind is too clouded to allow the realization that he will never achieve more than a distant second place to my true desire.

That his heart and soul are shielded by the mighty hand of God.

Pray hard against my promise that—for what was lost between our poetry in the night and your sanctioned broadcast of my availability in daylight—

someone must pay.

Love is a Bad, Bad Man

Nancy Jackson

Love is a bad, bad man
who finds a spark of interest in a woman's heart and fans it to a
flame of desire.

Who, swaddling her in darkness, feeds the fire with bits of tinder
and kindling—
fuel so quickly consumed it could easily have been imagined.

Long into the craftily constructed night, he keeps it burning,
until finally, growing bored with fighting off truth, he allows the
break of dawn.

She startles awake with tears of shame dousing what heat remains,
extinguishing the burning "why" on her lips before it can be
spoken.

Now frozen in bewilderment, she can only follow his remorseless
escape,
with eyes hollow and haunted by the tortured spirits of beautiful
dreams.

The Shopping List

Rosalyn Marhatta

His anger lay on the ground
splatted out in words
to blare in her ears
three days later.

She wrote on her shopping list: "earplugs"

She played the movie of word slaps
and door slams in her head
till it numbed every nerve
except
it squeezed the tears from her eyes.

She cleaned out closets of antipathy,
studying the plaid on his shirts
until she was dizzy with questions.

Then she tossed them in a pile for charity
although burning seemed like a better idea.

She wrote on her shopping list: "matches"

The sound of truth is a song
called "I Fall to Pieces."

She wrote on her shopping list: "crazy glue"

Straight Talk

Rosalyn Marhatta

I am a red slash across a black and white photo,
a tsunami of ocean,
an earthworm waiting for the hook
to impale her body,
the shortest distance from A to B,
the flight of a crow,
the path of an arrow aimed at a deer,
a knife cut across an apple pie,
thirteen silk stripes red and white
on the American flag
in a windstorm,
a steel wire used as a garrote,
a welt across a child's cheek,
the trail of a bullet headed for the heart,
a nerve frayed and split,
the rope in the tug of war
between lovers who spar outside a boxing ring
where an unrepentant Cupid laughs.

He Might Be a Beast

Coventry Kessler

He stands in immaculate white at the end of the hall,
laughing freely with nurses and patients, consulting with
    colleagues,
at perfect ease: the powerful, middle-aged doc.
He was kind during therapy, warmly peeking around the door:
    "Hello, dear!"
patiently explaining the regimen, asking how you felt, what
    problems you had,
discussing Kurasawa, Jane Austen, the pleasures of Chinese
    cooking,
listening by the bedside as you poured out your torrent of grief
until he snared your heart and tied it in the trap:
the longed-for love, the other half, the one you would have chosen
    if you could.

What do you know of him really, this kindly middle-aged doc
with the pretty wife and kids, the grand reputation,
who lights up others' eyes as they exclaim, "How wonderful he is!"
"How dedicated!" "How very kind!"?
What do the wife and children whisper
behind private walls, far from public praise:
The relentless tongue, the critical eye—
"Nothing is ever good enough!" The laughter at cherished dreams.
The abandoned bed. The railing against the world.
The scotch glass drained and toppled on the rug.
The absences past midnight. The looted bank accounts.
The belt that's used for more than tightening pants.
The bruises and cuts and blackened eyes of an injudicious word.
Worst: the disappearance into the child's room
when he thinks his pretty wife is fast asleep.

Too well you know the contrast of public and private.
Quake as you watch him stand in perfect beauty, ease, repute.
Fear that the world's bright angel transmutes
into the ravening beast.

The Shochet

Coventry Kessler

On the eve of asking for divorce

The shochet stands on the killing floor,
his blade upraised, tallit fringes dangling
above the stain of sacrifice pooled at his feet.
For a moment he bows his kippah-covered curls,
murmurs the ritual prayer, begs for death to arrive
in one clean, clear stroke:
mercy, sparing pain, as he takes life to sustain life.
Before him, the mild-eyed beast stands trusting, unawares.

I am standing at the kitchen sink, peeling potatoes,
cutting up the chicken for our supper.
My sons squabble, push, laugh as they fly down stairs
on their way to cartoons or Godzilla.
My husband says, "I found the microwave at Sears for 60 bucks."
"That's great," I reply, not looking up. He asks,
"How do you like the new dishwasher?"
From his parents' anniversary check, now far too late.
Microwave, dishwasher, recent repairs, all far too late.
"Oh, yes, it's fine," I say, still staring down. "It's just what we needed."
He seems unsure whether to be angry or mollified,
finds nothing else to say, leaves. Alone I watch
the chicken's helpless blood sluicing down the drain.

"Blessed are Thou, O Lord, Our God, King of the Universe,
Who has kept us and sustained us and brought us to this day:
Please, Lord, tomorrow: one clean, clear stroke."

Legacy

Susan Dean Wessells

With withering glance and scathing tongue you slide beneath the skin
of children, sons and daughters who, because they are your kin,
you think are yours to insult and abuse.

We think we shouldn't care and try to shrug it off, but know
that somewhere deep inside the tides of strong emotions flow,
which, damage done, bewilder and confuse.

And rage, like dynamite, is building up inside
until a sharp remark, a caustic one, or snide,
is all it takes to light the readied fuse.

Then we, with scathing glance and withering tongue, give tit for tat,
exploding now on you, the elders and the parents that
have left a legacy we can't refuse.

AROUND THE WORLD AND HOME

Apostrophe

Jean Rodenbough

"My name is Barack Obama, of the Moneygall Obamas, and I've come home to find the apostrophe we lost somewhere along the way."
>   —President Obama's opening lines to the crowd in
>   Dublin, Ireland

It's what got left behind somewhere
That relationship of word to meaning
The mystery of omission
It lingers still among the dullards
What's he hiding
What is missing

The lost generations of tribe
And clan and culture
Song and dance
Rhythms of the past
Stretches of trees
Across the savannahs
Dotting the earth's
Sweet smell
The smell of torn flesh
Of enemies speared
Of death
Cadence of calls to arms
Images of islands in blue seas
Ancestries in the Green Isle

Fill in the blanks
Fit the pieces in the puzzle
Left behind
Ignored
Unrewarded
Unacknowledged
Unbidden from pages
Of genealogies
Of grammar
The small curve
This connecting sign
With a hundred meanings
We simply say apostrophe

Tribute

Barbara Baillet Moran

for Melanie

You seem the perfect
California girl—born there, tall, slim,
moving like a dancer.
A model? Actress? No.

A stoic warrior heart beats within
your blue flight suit.
Weeks of boot camp gave you
that confident stride.

Still in adolescence, you
entered the world's dark heart
on that March day, part of the air cover
as convoys marched
over the border into Iraq.

Before you flew Black Hawks,
you donned that bulky suit, strode in the dust
to disarm roadside bombs, reached in
with your long fingers,
found the wires.

Later, you flew bomb squads into the minefields.
Some returned with you. Others did not.
Sometimes, your strafed craft barely landed at base
before falling apart.

Fire and Chocolate

Now, after twelve years and four deployments
to Iraq, Pakistan, and Afghanistan,
you are a civilian. Still flying,
you bring patients from remote areas,
land on the hospital roof.

But this is not the world you knew at eighteen.
Your youth lies stillborn
in the sand and blood of those desert lands.
The shapes and shadows of your nightscape
are alien and ugly.
Your band of brothers?
Scattered, wounded, blown up.

Today you say:
I don't fit in here.
I belong with my brothers.

In all ways but one,
you are with them still.

Behind the Dumpster

Cynthia Strauff Schaub

Behind the dumpster,
leaning:
"Richard Wayne Ammons, Marine."
Killed in the first Gulf war.
Who remembers that?

The flag folded,
a triangle.
His picture, smiling,
in uniform.

Who loved him?
Who tenderly framed
this memory?

And why, now,
not quite
in a dumpster?

Traveling the Silk Road

Judith Behar

Before Marco Polo,
before Christ or the Buddha,
we baked clay amphorae,
fermented grapes and honey,
ground seeds into spices.
Alphabets rattling, we loaded
our camels, our horses, our billowing ships:
traders, merchants, explorers,
we stamped paths into roads,
skimmed sea roads, then sky roads.

Rockslides, earthquakes,
tsunamis, volcanic eruptions
slowed us down,
stopped some dead
in tracks and vapor trails—
still we left home,
restless and jazzed, traveling
onward, always onward.

Now our artifacts squat
in glass cases in quiet museums,
our wanderings spelled out in placards
naming our homelands,
the places we traveled, the gods
we invoked. We have entered
history's long hallway
where the ring of bronze on steel
is silent, where the past
whispers in dead languages.

Who will walk on Mars? Who
will fly to the stars?

China Road

Caren Masem

Two boys in baskets
hang from a wooden yoke
borne by a woman, her head bent
forward. Her dusty black hair
sways over hunched shoulders.

One child hangs on two-handed,
tight-fisted, stubborn, as his vessel tilts.
He will soon separate from the woman
who carried him close to her body
only months before.

All our sons must leave our arms
and make their way on the road,
dusty and rocky,
dusty and rocky.

A Visitor

Anya Russian

      For Lih's mother

Shuffling between kitchen and living room,
she carries trays of sliced mangoes,
salted rice patties, and red bean sweets,
a crown of utility carefully balanced
over tragedy's swiveling door.
She opens the paper wrappings,
hands delicate as a crocus unfolding
in the morning light. Little hands working
to part the frail chapter of circumstance
where histories float like clouds on an untouchable scrim.
A husband long dead and children long grown,
she hums now in perpetual migration
strummed by memories quiet as dusk—
notes plucked from hills overgrown with simple reasons
prying her open as stars from distant galaxies
pierce the silent circumference of night.
How roots cling to raked earth
and a culture slides down a mountain
into the heart-shaped contours of her lips
settling there in soft syllables
that ripen in her smile like tomatoes
in the scalding Taiwanese sun.
She courts her years, still a child playing dress-up,
desire toted like a feather hat or an afterthought;
a parasol sprouts from the tiny bulb of her hand,
and her eyes follow with unintended curiosity
as the palm leaves flap their giant
destinies in the window.

Walking the Line

Anya Russian

I buy taro root on the roadside,
dirty bulbs still clinging to the
familiar underground.

Locals, barefoot,
stare out of a squat doorway,
a boarded shack barely
hanging onto the pleated edge
of a mountain,
at the windows of the minibus
as our faces fly by like pictures
flipped in a comic book,
watching the way you would a snail
in an aquarium—attentive,
        but unconcerned.

The tilted universe between us.

I seek a thoroughfare, a break, a dotted line,
   a depression.

Like a broad-shouldered vase
inquiring towards its slender neck,

I crave proximity—
the full shadowed sphere of the moon
hiding behind its crescent suggestion.

I want to unclench the jaw
of our well trained synapses
suturing this gold sputtering moment.

To spear the tongue chained
to some mental command
and its ridiculous notations.

To tackle the army of failed
language and incalculable gesture
that gathers like a wave in the ocean,
folding in upon itself,
making a fool of intention.

My smile startles like a hiccup,
brackets me in my own sentence.

These words float into rings of smoke,
impossible O's that nestle themselves
in the wide potholes grinning
under a blanket of orange dust.
So we are reduced to routine transactions—
the bloated sun rising and setting
its same steady ordinance,
our perspiration continuing
its long labor to the ground,
the comforting gait of our inhalations
and exhalations,

the body's unifying standard—

the straight, bold, flat line
seesawing between us.

— *Laos*

How Black My Valley

Muriel Hoff

Before the Communists came
to Copsa Mica, Romania,
Franti Teclas churned milk
to make a soft white cheese
and sold it in the village.
The sheep were white,
the grass green,
the flowers scarlet and yellow,
the houses red, blue, and brown.

For Franti Teclas,
nature's gifts filled
her life with simple
pleasures.

After the Communists came
to Copsa Mica, Romania,
the factory spewed smoke,
showered the sheep with soot.
A black blanket covered
the flowers, grass, houses.

For Franti Teclas,
nature's gifts filled
her life with black
shadows.

After Communism collapsed
in Copsa Mica, Romania,
the factory closed.
The sheep were again white,
the grass green, flowers
scarlet and yellow and
the houses red, blue, brown.

For Franti Teclas,
nature's gifts returned.
Time to churn the milk
to make a soft white cheese.

After the bulletins were posted
in Copsa Mica, Romania,
Franti Teclas read:
Don't eat the sheep.

Don't eat the vegetables
from your garden.
Don't drink the water.
Poison in the soil and food chain:
Pollutants, lead, zinc, cadmium.

For Franti Teclas,
nature's gifts again a sinful sham;
simple pleasures now bittersweet
memories.

Child of War: A Memory

Diana Engel

"There is no good war and no small journey."
—Peter Machuak, Lost Boy of Sudan

Night:
I heard the army
marching, advancing
closer to my house,
my goats slaughtered,
bleating,
the dry sizzle of fire
burning grass.
Mama ran into my room
with a cup of cool water,
dressed me in cotton shirt and pants,
pushed me out the door
into the jungle.

Screams from my village grew
fainter as I raced farther
into the trees.
My mother, father, sister—
I prayed they ran.
Don't leave me alone in this dark night.

Into the bush
I hurried,
became night the way
the lizard becomes the tree.
I had to get to Ethiopia.

For weeks I walked
as my heels cracked, bled.
I tore my shirt to bind them.
Sleeping on Sudan's rugged crags,
I lay as still as a turtle in its shell,
prayed that the lion would not maul me.

Through killing bush,
then scorching desert
I pushed despair
into my rumbling belly,
fed it hard, dusty roots
and muddy Nile water.
Memory, a hungry predator,
returned as the Sahara moon rose:
stalking my mind,
devouring my heart.

I remembered Papa coming after me,
laughing into the savannah,
Mama cradling me in her arms, singing "hush,"
Sister and my friends
kicking a red ball
across the village playground.

Gone.
My searching heart,
my home.

One Purple African Dusk

Catherine Ashley-Nelson

One purple African dusk in dry season
I sat outside my blue-louvered door
on straw mat spread
across concrete slab of porch
and milked the beauty from twilight,
watched bats flit by
and dip to nip the insects of night
near my skin-warmed hair.

Then I heard the beating of drums:
irresistible, soul-spawned sounds
that spanned millennia,
nudged ancestral memory.

I rose to my sandaled feet,
like a child seduced by the Hamelin flute,
trailing the tail of my wrapped skirt,
crossed the dusty yard,
passed through my gate,
followed the music
down the broad dirt street
till I reached the darkening shade
of a frangipani and a flame tree
by the open sewer growing side by side.

There five children, as young as three,
not older than twelve,
beat with bare hands and sticks
on plastic buckets, a battered oil drum,
two hubcaps, and one empty paint can.
They saw me standing there, enrapt,
appreciated even an audience of one.
Tempo escalated, fingers flew,
heads bobbed, shoulders punctuated phrasing.

I applauded in humble respect, this music
that spoke of rainy seasons and droughts,
of plantings and harvests, dances and dancers.

As I walked home, their rhythms
softening with distance, the beauty of
night and music too much to bear,
I cried for some indefinable time and space,
perhaps some subconscious moment
in the Arizona desert of my childhood
where the outdoors was often my bedroom,
where coyotes made wild music in the night,
where playthings were old broomsticks and spent tires.

And I cried for a friend who had left
the country just days before,
deprived of the purple remnants of sunset,
now swallowed up,
and of this Sahelian night
on Chadian soil.

But then I looked up
at the cloudless, moonless sky,
shameless with stars, and I smiled.
The boys had no need of my applause.
They had a celestial audience
and they performed in a packed arena.

Ode to the Confederate Monument

Jean Rodenbough

("Turn your eyes to the immoderate past . . .")*

The centuried monument, landmark,
sustained its denouement
before dawn broke upon the city:
the van's powerful drive into the center
of the traffic circle.
The Soldier was toppled, broken
into pieces, fifteen of them, with the head
embedded in the van.
The driver fell asleep at 4:30 a.m. on his way
home. Disasters will happen, we know.
Such as a war.

One hundred years it stood
in honor of the Confederate dead.
Now it lies in pieces.
Comments and controversy follow.
"It will take a while to get it restored,"
advised the United Daughters
of the Confederacy spokeswoman.

Let the unintended
pre-dawn moment be a gift and opportunity.
"The ragged arms, the ragged heads and eyes,"*
honored at last in the breach.

*From "Ode to the Confederate Dead" by Allen Tate

Fire and Chocolate

Walk Through Battleground

Sandra Redding

This is where our history began.
Here, beneath the pine needles
and red clay soil
rest the bones of soldiers
who fought so we could trek
this bountiful trail.

We salute the battle-scarred image
of General Greene,
study the determined faces
of other sculpted heroes:
who we are.

Hiking on past oaks and birches,
we smile, believing this place
blessed with laurel
and passionflowers
was created *only for us*.

Startled, we look up,
witness the fleeting beauty
of rushing deer.

Linden Tree

Diana Engel

for Zachary Christopher McMillan—Uncle Chris

Fifty years ago,
my young uncles
watched a storm drive clods
of dirt from gnarled roots.

Mini balls and lead bullets,
Civil War relics long hidden
emerged.

Pretend soldiers,
they grabbed these prizes
with wonder
as the heart-shaped leaves
streamed tears of rain.

Freedom

Don Webb

Freedom.
You can taste it, but it's not there.
There are many prisons,
none worse than the mind.
Caged thoughts, hampered spirits, restrained hope.
The only relief is sleep,
but it comes less and less.
How can someone be in such a dark place and still see?
The bars of your cell are shadow lines.
You can see through them,
but not past them.
That's the true torture of prison—
Freedom.

Betty Sue Waits Tables at the Waffle House in Madison, Alabama

Janice L. Sullivan

I know I sound like a machine
spitting out orders but when
a fella like that man sits
at the counter, fourth stool over

I ask him if he wants
the same and he nods.
I holler to the cook, "Ham and cheese,
fries and sweet tea."

Well, la de da, here comes
a family all dressed up.
They slide into one of our
red booths and pull out
a menu, talk over their orders.

The son, skinny as a lost greyhound,
orders two waffles, two sausage patties,
three scrambled eggs, grits, and a Coke.

The father orders scrambled eggs, bacon,
grits, and coffee. The mother with a big diamond ring
asks for one egg over medium, wheat toast,
tomatoes, and decaffeinated coffee.
That's not enough to feed a baby chicken.

When I bring the family their orders,
the woman stares at my new tattoo.
She touches her egg, points
out that it is not firm enough.
Would you cook it a little longer?
Yes, of course, we aim to please.

Oh well, I smile a big one.
One waitress yells, "Beep-beep,"
signals for that new thin girl
to get out of her way . . . now.

Mama wants me to look for
another job. She says that it is
time for me to move up. I tell her
I'm with family and I am just fine.

The County Library

Walt Pilcher

I found a place you've gotta see,
Down in the valley 'bout a mile from me.
It's called the County Library,
And you can take home books for free!
Yeah, you can take home books for free
Down at the County Library!

There's books and magazines galore
On the shelves and on the floor.
There's comfy chairs and a whole lot more,
And you can smoke outside the door.
There's books on tape and DVDs
Down at the County Library.

The ladies at the desk are nice,
But mind your manners is my advice.
Too much noise will sure suffice
To throw you out like you got lice.
So don't annoy the powers that be,
Down at the County Library.

Check out all those books for free,
But you gotta bring them back, you see.
Forgot one time so I stood in line;
But all they said was, "That's a fine!"
Well, if it's fine with them, it's fine with me,
Down at the County Library.

Browse the Internet; there's no fee.
Look for a job or buy a TV.
There's no telling what you'll see,
But the racy sites are blocked (whew-ee),
So it's safe for the kids and the family,
Down at the County Library.

Fire and Chocolate

Out back they've got a Book-Mobile.
It used to be a real big deal.
They say it lost its curb appeal, but
The whole idea's so surreal:
There's books with wheels? Well, glory be!
Down at the County Library.

They hired a man with a funny name;
They lose a book, he gets the blame.
Like to meet him, but he can't be found;
Old Dewey Decimal's not around.
He's hiding systematically,
Down at the County Library.

Well, there's Borders, and Walden, and Amazon,
Barnes, and Noble, and Books dot com,
Target, and Wal-Mart, and even eBay.
Only thing is . . . You gotta pay!
Don't need a literary shopping spree
When you can get your books for free,
Down at the County Library.

Starbucks has its points, I guess,
But it's sure not cheap, and it's not the best.
Hot water from the Men's Room—free—
Makes my coffee, instantly.
And, well, that's good enough for me,
Down at the County Library.

Can't use my cell phone, that's no go.
Disturbs the other folks, you know.
So leave a message at the beep and
Here's a promise I might keep:
Call you soon as I am free
When I get home from the Library.

Learn new words, impress your friends.
They'll think you've been to school again.
So flaunt your tax-paid education,
Grammar and pronunciation,
Like you got a P. H. Dee,
Down at the County Library.

Now when I quit this mortal zoo—
Check out before I'm overdue—
Don't picture me in death's embrace…
Just put a bookmark in my place,
Down at the County Library.
Down at the County Library.

Check it out!

GROWING UP,
GROWING OLD

High School

Cynthia Strauff Schaub

Grey skirt,
grey blazer,
maroon tie.
Remember?
And, oh, having that TPS* pin in
just the right spot,
holding collar tight, upright.

All unspoken, of course,
but observed,
copied.

Socks too.
Wool, bleached yellow,
almost tatty—to a limit.

A straight jacket? Or
learning the
way of the world
in an egg of nuns,
hidden cigarettes, and
algebra?

*Trinity Preparatory School

Molly's Clay Pot

Janice L. Sullivan

She turns the urn, feels grains
of sand from a creek bed,
sees wrinkles folded in the clay.

A large pot, dark as swamp mud,
it is a safe vessel for memories,
those from her grandmother.

Like her life, there is roughness
and smoothness in this vessel.
When she holds it, she remembers

walks along the edge of the pond.
With bare feet, she felt ridges
of wet mud under her toes.

She recalls playing *kick the can*,
running too hard, stirring up dust,
making her mama's face turn red.

Don't Call Me an Old Bag

Muriel Hoff

I am a Hermes bag.
Like the Gods I am eternal.
I am valued by rich society women
and envied by poor working girls.

My skin is supple and never wrinkles.
My accessory parts are memorable,
original, one of a kind.

I reside at the most exclusive
high fashion shops.
I am often displayed in the window accompanying
a mannequin's dress, suit, or other
piece of clothing by a famous designer.

I have appeared in the advertisements
of international haute couture magazines.
The model is always beautiful, but I am
the main attraction.

Working girls save their money for years
so they can possess me.
I heard that in Tokyo a young secretary slept
with me in her bed when her boyfriend left her.

If someone tires of me I can be sold to
an exclusive vintage shop.
My price always remains in the higher brackets.
I'm worth it.

The Recycling of Sadye

Muriel Hoff

They waltzed across the Atlantic:
Sadye in sequined chemise,
Herman in rented tuxedo.
Herman's ashes now rest in the
porcelain urn on the mantel.

Sadye pushes the battered carriage
filled with empty beer cans,
Schlitz, Stroh's, Miller,
gleaming in the Miami sunshine,
guarded by a gray-headed, rouged lady.

The children call her Aunt Sadye.
She brings them chocolate kisses.
The cats purr, dogs wag tails
as she forages through the garbage pails,
meandering down back streets and alleys.

Aunts

Jane Gibson Brown

Antimacassars, give me antimacassars
and aunts, in faded purple clothes
with sagging seams and baggy hose,
aunts with sturdy, hard-rock bones,
seated by fires,
flashing fingers knitting
warm scarves or throws.
They people hotels and homes,
with canes go to Sunday church,
Miss Agnes or Miss Kate in name;
they have the courage still to shame
the guilty. Where are those aunts
insisting on castor oil
or mustard plasters to boil?
No one can hold herself
as straight in lace
or so sensibly wear grace
as those venerable old creatures
with time's stuffing spilling out.

Mobile Meals

Lois Losyk

Carrying a meager meal and drink,
I climb out of my car.
Fear grips me as two yard dogs,
teeth bared, bark warnings.
Heavy chains strain as they lunge
to attack me.
I pray they hold.

Three sad cars bearing telltale signs
of better days watch from the weeds
and tall grass.

I walk up to what is left of a tiny house
crumbling in on itself,
dying a slow death of neglect
along with its owner.
Mrs. Hart sits in the open doorway
flashing a toothless smile.
Her eyes runny, each looking a different way,
as if there is too much
to see in just one direction.

Two cats circle around me. "Strays,"
she says. "They just abandon them and
I feed the poor starving things."

She takes the meal and thanks me.
Suddenly her face lights up.
"I'm 88 today," she beams
 like a proud child turning six.
"How wonderful," I say.

I head back to my car thinking
of this difficult, heartless world.
Mrs. Hart knows.

It's wonderful to be alive.

When I Retire

Jane Gibson Brown

When I retire
I want a band
to play me out
with a drummer
whose staccato beat
is as crisp and cool
as the starch in
the finality of my dress.
I want no words
in this jazzy affair,
just music, maybe dancing,
until we, all in, fall
each in a chair
dry mouthed and gasping,
and no breath left
to sigh a goodbye.
We'll just toddle off
to waiting cars
and drive into
the late night
with the music
still in our ears.

Woodcut of an Old Woman

Lynne Martin Bowman

Once my words took a turn
and I could not find them—
see how I bend over the ploughed rows,
the field upturned and new,
ready for the seed, ready for the water,
ready for the blessing which will not come.
I am a shadow against the sun,
the silhouette in the carving.
See how the rings round the sun,
jagged cuts in the wood;
now deep ink marks light
and thick paper keeps the day.
Even if I knew what the harvest would bring,
I would work the clodded land.
The cuts tell the story,
my telling went before me,
and soon into the furrow
I followed.

Crooked Old Dogs

Caren Masem

Old dogs, when you look at them,
never seem quite straight.
Their two front legs are always
to the left or to the right of their back legs.
I wonder how this happens.
If humans were like this, I could see why.
We always have one hip out,
especially women.
There's always a baby perched
on a hip thrown out to the side,
or a bag of groceries that, while awfully heavy,
may not contain enough
to go around the table.
And, at the last, years spent sinking
in an old mattress with stained ticking
and hard metal buttons rearranges
our bodies, if not our souls too.

Washing His Glasses I Think

Caren Masem

Through these lenses he sees me.
I wash the glass gently.
Soapy water runs over
and between my fingers,
then in rivulets down the rims.
I hold the frames up to the light
that streams in the window
above the kitchen sink.

Thoughts wander to what he sees—
a woman changing every day,
less tall, less sturdy, more broad,
more forgetful of the kindnesses
for which she once had strength.

His power too, diminished.
His domain much smaller
as he survives but does not win
battles with younger men.

I see his dreams fade away,
covered in clouded years.

Autumn Trek

Sandra Redding

Hiking Poet's Walk in Hillsborough,
the old man stoops down, scoops up muscadines.
As he shares this winy sacrament with his wife,
the west wind howls. Shivering trees
surrender coats of amber, red, magenta.

Pausing to rest beside the unstill water,
the woman bites into a juicy apple
and passes it to her husband.
"It won't be long now," she says.
"Yes," he agrees. "It won't be long."

Nearing the end, he points his cane.
"Up ahead, there's a graveyard."
His wife avoids the somber view.
"And just beyond stands the mansion," he says.

Cold despite their padded jackets, they trudge on.
Above them, black wings gather against a stormy sky.

On Not Having Children

Stephen G. Wessells

How I impoverish the days to come
having no son; the future has a hole
one daughter deep, and that is infinite!
What fear has left me lonely in my age
so youth could prance unfettered? From the past
my young self leers, for it shall not be he
who faces death with no posterity.
The dangers I dodged would have made me strong
had I but faced them, and my shallow love
dug deep into those cancelled generations.
No regretting now; I cannot feel
that hand not quite my own touching my own
to ease my tottering steps toward my end,
or, standing at the shore when my mind sinks
into senility, tossing a line.
My choices, like my future, are all mine.

Mother's Healing

Ellen Summers

In her late bad days,
my mother was a glass
of turbid fluid,
roiled and fouled in a rage
of fear: through her
light could not pass
but hovered
in the murky cage;

but when she was still, breathed
evenly, the clay
sank, bit by bit, and cleared
the water, till at last
the glass glittered in light,
pure and precious draft;
and it was right

that when we came to take her
empty body, we saw
nothing but dregs.
That very day

one who longed
for her had called
her back to the sea, called
all her waters home,
where now she swims
in light.

I hear her singing,
indigo summer nights,
heartbeats slow,
breaths evening.

BELIEVING

Call to Prayer

Anya Russian

Every evening one star emerges
from the hazy field of lilac
seeding some law of nature
into night's impartial descent.
The brightly painted houses
pose by the stiff rows of palm trees,
a tricycle abandoned on the sidewalk,
an empty bench, kneel like embers
under the quiet, bright loneliness.
Somewhere a mosque points
its needled dome towards the sky.
The shadows widen their grip
with the mosquitoes' crescendo,
and something burns, something pure melts—
the call to prayer, scratchy and feeble,
crawls through speakers
into the humid air—

welcome stranger beginning a new conversation
welcome rose unfolding
warm cloak disrobing
oil in the grooves
sap running down the tree
reveal the lies of the day, the treads in the road
harness our steam for your intimate publication
the mellow, aching tenor of the bloodstream
the soft feel of flour falling through the fingers
the sad incense of the temporal
opening a cave deep inside that knows
this sentry of a mind huddled by the fire
tending to a meek flame

that star pinned like a third eye
to its galaxy, its hemisphere
to the solemn melody
drifting us someplace between truth
and the imagination.

— *Malaysia*

It is Not You Alone

Coventry Kessler

(Adapted from the *Siddur*)

It is not you alone who pray
Or we or they
All things pray
All things pour forth their souls to God
The heavens pray and the earth
Every creature and every living thing
In all of life, longing dwells
Creation itself a prayer to the Almighty
What are the clouds
The rising and the setting sun
The soft radiance of the moon
The gentleness of night
The flashes of the mind
The storms of the human heart
But prayers, all prayers
As we pour forth
Our boundless longing for God

Thanksgiving Eve 1992

Coventry Kessler

The scent of cinnamon and ginger, nutmeg and clove,
redolent of ancient East, adventurers' caravans seeking far,
hovers above my stove,
stealing its way through my children's hair, floating on midnight pillows,
turning their eager, sleep-struck faces toward the pleasures of
tomorrow:
Twin pumpkin pies, round and merry as foxes' eyes,
two fat and warty squashes, gone to their just desserts.

Outside the windowsill, the modest oak tree shivers in the rain.
The beech, leaves bright as copper pennies, federal coins for stolen
land,
stands Indian-still, ghost-man trapped in grey, sinewous bark,
silent testament to those rooted in earth before.

The mist descends. The air hangs still. The cat,
illicitly on table, stretches, yawns, licks luxurious paws,
then leaps beside my leg, cruising to and fro in mellifluous pleading:
Milk, please—hold the honey—
lapping the fat of the land,
the thrum of her satisfied throat
a prayer of Thanksgiving.

sacrifice

A. C. Hardy

the night
is cold and still

clouds
hang like effigies
in forgotten dreams

the telegraph-T of the lines
bear witness
to your dying

i think nothing equal to love
has yet been found

an ancient tree
groans in the distance

and i imagine you hanging there
desperate and alone

sacrament

A. C. Hardy

broken
I
imagine
You
taking
it all
inside

savoring
each
bitter
morsel
of life

in a
eucharist
of pain

knowing
Your betrayer
in a pact
with God
had sealed
Your fate

At San Damiano

Jean Rodenbough

the trees
through high glass windows
we watch them and the way
they bend and twist from the earth
California live oaks and rouge-marked Madrones
rough-barked, cross-trunked
they lean to the dining room
we eat here beside the great trees

meditation walk
quiet
only the shuffled sound of sandals
the silence covers even softest thoughts
in this line of walkers
as we enter the chapel
our meditations merge into the bright
day of prayer and singing
music strings our petitions together
a necklace of words

gates
we know to close gates
wrought-iron security from deer
who crave the flowers in tamed
gardens where the once wild
outside is held by earth inside
we have no choice
lest the intruders enter
and eat all the pretty colors
the green and the red
blue and lavender—succulent
flavors lure longing creatures—
flower Sirens call to Odyssean deer
tempting tastes for their tongues
we close the gate with a sharp click!

Where Have You Been All Of My Life?

Lois Losyk

I ran into God
the other day.
Unexpectedly.

He walked alongside me
in the woods that cool blue
morning, His presence
heavy in the air.

*Where have you been
all of my life?*

He didn't speak
but I heard
every word:

*In the lilies of the pond
as they greet the day,
their white faces turned
upward to bathe in the warmth
of the morning sun.*

*In a baby's laugh
that sprinkles
its confetti
in your heart.*

*In your dog's soulful eyes
when he lays his head
in your lap.*

*When the cardinal sits
on a tree branch singing:
Right here. Right here.*

The Present

Nancy Jackson

So it begins:

Grand yellow blossoms lift their chins to greet their namesake.

Countless tiny spiderlets cast their fate on a warm updraft
to prepare the loom of day with a warp of silver.

Lithe stems of crepe myrtle bow under the weight of
amethyst crowns, still twinkling with captured starlight.

The ancient maple beckons, "Come share my cool, patient peace.
Come worship from within this mighty temple
walled with fluttering panes of stained glass."

Marvel as the moist veins of a freshly fallen leaf are
revealed by the light to be lined with gold dust.

Applaud the frenzied Fairies' Reel of dragonflies on the wing.

Revel in the chickadee's insistent invitation to a
dance of tag with the dappling shadows.

Delight in spying the hummingbird, rising from its rest
perched delicately at eye level.

Grin with glee at the squirrel's arrogant dangling
before the cat's limit of reach and speed.

Glimpse the blush of the doves caught in naughty pleasure.

There, amidst the din of the waking wild—
the peal no church bells can rival—
I lift my voice with the host of children
so loved by God, He prepared this gift of a summer morning
to follow a midnight rain.

DEATH AND LOSS

River at the End of Day

Lynne Martin Bowman

A fog rises from the river that might run at the back of the yard,
the compost hiding it. Those bits of leaf and flower, warm with rot,
cook the air just so water hangs its shreddy misty clothes along the
    fence.
Are you riding there? Speaking in a whisper just softer than the doves
at evening, disappearing in the bleed of daylight. Just as three or four
    stars
rise, I cannot tell which is the first—wishes blur to fence lines, the last
bird sounds, the fading etch of sycamore and oak. Your death was no
    tragedy,
you simply died, like anyone who is old and hollowed out fades into the
    night.
I could not stop it, would not, did not want to keep you from that
    calling;
I only wanted you to be my father still, my father in his bronze hour, sun
at late day spilling across the sinuate waves, my father with his pole in
    hand,
his boat, his black dog waiting.

Where My Father is Buried I Have Not Been

Lynne Martin Bowman

That place withdrawing with the late sun
I long for, but cannot go. The grey stone
shadows the light; the light, such docile fingers
now, cannot touch the etched words, words
blurring to granite, granite fading into grass,
grass merging into the soft dark that always comes.

I imagine it is difficult for the bones to get used
to disappearing, the lift of wind so hard to navigate,
to be tumbled like a stone being polished or
a weed being torn from its root—polished until
there is only shine, torn until there is only dust,
and even those bright bits swallowed black.

How the night is made of these particles,
touching us, yet we cannot see. Why is he wearing
his raincoat in my mother's dreams? Where is he
going, has he gone? The particles form and disperse,
form and disperse—What do we know? Waves
slur in and back, ruffle the sand with shell and stone.
I only hope he can find home when he needs it,
knows us when he sees us.

Playing the Odds

Fran Ostasiewski

At age eleven, I had an operation. I was never told that I would likely die during the surgery, nor that I would not see seventeen without it. Forty-three years later the images remain: the intense illumination forcing my eyes into narrow slits, the cold unyielding silver table, strangers in green pajamas, masks and beanies unrolling sleeping bags of shiny instruments—many were knives, the rough wiping as they attached wires to my skin and the beginning "beep beep beep beep." More alarming was the black cup surrounded by fingertips emerging from the light above me. Did I scream "stop" as it touched my face, or, was I just thinking out loud?

a steel trap
alongside the pond
three footprints

Bodies and Bones

Gail Barger

The back yard is littered
with bodies and bones:
cats, dogs, squirrels,
mice and a bunny or two,
most still in their skin.
Every night I gather
them up
and bring them in.
The sun rises,
morning comes,
the back door opens
and one by one
the bodies and bones
get carried out again.

Sweeping

Gail Barger

Still, crisp, sweet,
the scent of candied apples,
and burning leaves in the air.
Fall dropping into the South.

One of us swept the kitchen,
the other made the bed,
diligently devoted to our labor.
Our play, our reverie.

Dirt floors scraped bare,
we raked low leafy walls
into room-sized squares,
open spaces, windows, and doors.

The forest, our furniture store—
a hollow log became a sofa,
our table, a board on a stack of stones,
a plump pile of leaves our bed.

Fall faded, wind blew,
night came early, windows frosted.
Winter tossed a lacey white spread.
Our house lumps and bumps beneath.

Slashing the forest, a new highway
swept us into the world.
Dried leaf playhouse, a puff of dust
beneath our sprouting wings.

Fire and Chocolate

Fledgling fliers unaware,
we were never again as free and safe,
as inside the walls
of our swept-leaf home.

A raven patrolled a fiery sky,
talons flexed in melting sun.
One of us survived, the other done.

A Casualty Delayed

Ellen Summers

Although I wasn't there the day they cut
my brother's body down,
I was, the next week, when we came to put
his body in the ground.
The dead aren't always in the earth, you know.
Sometimes they rise,
sometimes they wither while alive, and go
with shuttered eyes
about their ordinary rounds, the noose
already round their throat.
My brother's hold on life was far too loose:
he seemed to float.
He'd thought of dying since he was thirteen.
That was the year
my father died when climbing a ravine
in a glacier;
they cut his body free and shipped it back:
his oldest son
still felt suspended in the hanging wrack
until cut down.

Dark Offspring

Susan Dean Wessells

Thirteen years
since I carried the dark offspring

It grew so quietly

Then
a crimson rush of blood
announced its presence

Twenty-eight days
I was aware
pregnant
with a tumor
nestled in my sorrowing womb
where no child, now, would grow

A month
of glorious autumn
tinged with ominous gray

Uncertainty
regarding if I would live
or die

Until the shining scalpel
like a valiant champion's blade

Invaded me

And, deft and sure,
carried the bleak malignant one away

Cherub

Rosalyn Marhatta

Tiny cherub
who runs through my life,
I hear your laughter
echoing from outside
as your brother pushes your swing.

Your glee resounds
throughout the house
and I bake your favorite brownies
without nuts.
"Nuts are yucky," you say.

I hear your small feet clomping
on the floor
and the dog barks
as your brother chases you, shouting,
"Give that back."

You clutch the marble in your hand,
holding it like an Olympic medal.
"You can't catch me," you say.

Your black curls fly
up, your jeans tear when you fall
but you pick yourself up
and keep running,
pushing your big brother
to the floor,
never letting go of that prize,
that bit of glass.
"Mine," you say.

The next day, death
drives onto the sidewalk,
whiskey at the wheel,
tires screech slamming you down;
I run to grab your hand.

The ambulance shrieks
on a ride as long as the Amazon River;
my tears boil over, apparitions of black ink
bend my mind, punch air out of my lungs.
I block death with screams
but he will not be denied.

Now the kitchen smells of brownies,
your brother presses your marble
into my hand. The wind
pushes the swing.

haunted

A. C. Hardy

what dreams
tonight
dear one

what shadows
follow you down
the paths of sleep

where ghosts
I cannot see
still haunt the darkness?

Portent

Stephen G. Wessells

Dark-winged as the angel of foreboding,
a buzzard woos the wind; wings barely shift,
each feather splayed to grasp a lilt of lift—
so effortlessly buoyant on the air
as if the earth were something hardly there,
a dream to hook the shadow of his drift
and anchor it to nesting ground, lest, floating
as an abstract word on the wind's breath,
he should forget that he must dine on death.

. . . and then the dark

Jean Rodenbough

we should know by now
should know that seasons
move us from light into dark
move us from there to where
we stand below this memory

remember how it has been for you
the days of love and friends and hope
that come before the forlorn winter
lifts its despair on twisted limbs
and blends into the deepening dark

remember how a new season appears
bringing less dark and more light
even as twilight cloaks the sky
first the single stars followed close
by more brilliance until with dawn
they vanish outshone by the sun

the winter's tree knows its will
knows how the wind blows
holds firm to the earth its roots
tight and tangled beneath the soil
while waiting for the rains of spring
the fresh plumage upon its branches
knows there is a season before the season
of darkness and the nothingness that waits

ART, WRITING, AND
ALL THAT JAZZ

That's Jazz

Julius Howell

Pour me slowly.
Take your time.
My skin, stretched thin—
Then, chords unwind.

Sip me gently—
Sour 'n sweet.
Dipped tongue drips echoes
after beat.

Hold me lightly.
Let me breathe.
For me to love you,
give me wings.

Hug me tightly.
Feel my burn.
You let me leave,
I won't return.

Empty mem'ries.
Drink me up—
the horns, the keys,
the strings, the drums.

The subtle buzz
of pure pizzazz—
that Funk, that Blues,
that Swing . . . That's Jazz.

Daingerfield's *Moonlight* at the Mint Museum

Diana Engel

Between earth-rooted globes of green
an opal orb hangs.

> long
> lonely
> deep
>
> Night

Snow at Giverny

Diana Engel

No longer in a climate-
controlled gallery, stalking
paintings along the perimeter,
a world of well-defined geometric
rooms framed on the exterior
by sidewalk paths,
stone fountain . . .

We arrive unawares in Giverny,
squinting through the eye of a winter
tornado that shields the nearest farmhouse
in a whirling, white cloak.
The storm a driving snow-wind.
Our summer bronzed arms and legs shiver,
sandaled feet packed under layers of ice.
Teetering back and forth like flimsy rag dolls,
we struggle in this landscape
endless, frozen.
Suddenly, wet thick bristles entrap us.
We dissolve.

Still Life in Orange and Blue

Janice L. Sullivan

First Friday Night, Bristol Gallery opens.
Alice paints azalea pink and lemon yellow,
colors of cottages in Portugal. She puts
her brush down, steps away from her easel.
I tell her her houses are bright as yesterday's
sunset at Pawley's Island.

One painting, brilliant orange and blue
like a soft, sweet mango, keeps luring
me back. My husband stands beside me,
says that *Still Life* reminds him of
Cezanne's *Apples and Oranges*.

At home he hands me a package
wrapped in thick, blue bubble wrap.
He smiles as he wishes me Happy Anniversary.
Each day, we sit in the breakfast room,
watch the finches eat from green bird feeders.
Next to the window hangs our new painting.
We imagine Cezanne sitting at our table.

Eudora Welty Came To Dinner

Barbara Baillet Moran

one spring evening. Her host,
anticipating lively, even brilliant talk,
assembled all manner of literati.
Writers, professors of English,
a Welty scholar filled the table,
Miss Welty at its head,
hapless host at its foot.

As salad plates were removed,
the meal's fate was already sealed.
Conversation was to be—limited.
Each male guest, revered by his students,
dared not ask an imperfect question, state the obvious,
aver a commonplace—before his peers.
No, he must watch and wait.

Laughter, jolly chatter from nearby tables
crushed the chosen, miserable few.
At last, the divine Eudora, in her eighties,
on a demure white horse at full gallop,
reined in at the table and reigned,
thereby saving the huddled mass
from further excruciation.

She spoke, her voice first a rivulet
rippling over pebbles and mossy mounds,
then a trilling mockingbird who well
understood the comedy unspooled below.
She told stories, spoke of her life,
asked about the work of others. Her
pure heart warmed worried souls, allowed
even poor host to breathe again. All questions,
every comment, they now knew, would be perfect.

Dessert was chocolate and the first raspberries of spring.

Little Women

Catherine Ashley-Nelson

So my friend says, out of the blue,
"What novel would you vote the best,
one that made the biggest impression on your life?"
Surprised, my lethargic mind, suddenly in panic,
time-travels back to college days,
to all those Russians, Brits, and U.S. Southerners
who now come trampling with muddy boots
through the pinhole of my memory:
Dostoevsky, Tolstoy, Nabokov,
Dickens, Thackeray, Conrad, all those Brontë gals,
Faulkner, Welty, Flannery O'Connor—
so easy to remember the love, so easy to forget the plots.

"*Crime and Punishment? War and Peace?
The Sound and the Fury?*" I offer tentatively,
amusing myself with the structural sameness.
He is quiet for a moment
as though trying to be thoughtful,
to give me some credit for intelligence,
though I know he favors contemporary fare,
is someone fond of John Grisham.
But just as a cat lands in my lap,
timely closing our discussion,
I realize I've lied, even with that awesome trio.

For it was another novel I remember best
though my literary mind could not confess it—
that first one I ever read—in the 4th, 5th, or 6th grade.
I still see Jo scribbling on her notepad,
almost feel her breath on my face, keenly remember
how the world seemed to change inside my head.
On those pages fell the first tears written words
ever brought me. How could she forego the devotion
with which Laurie loved her, turn down his proposal?

Jo was the one this same child heart admired for thinking
that writing was a real road one might walk down,
the same heart that cheered her for her ambitions, her dreams.

I remember how the little poems I scribbled
suddenly seemed to sprout wings,
beg to fly as high as the sky,
though they had no place to go—
except back under my pillow
where I kept them hidden.

The Writer

Cynthia Strauff Schaub

I write so beautifully at night
in my bed
in my head.
Really.
The words flow, pregnant and poignant—
poems, stories, fiction and non.
I am talented. What a gift!
Really.

As good as Dickinson, Oliver.
Look out,
Collins and Rilke,
Alice Munro, Barbara Pym.
I've learned from you.
I am that deep.

So why, when morning comes,
am I
ordinary?

The Poet

A. C. Hardy

I

in the salt-mine desert
of dreams
you have hidden your shame

pure crystalline
gem stones

waiting to be mined

II

in caverns
of night
dreams
coalesce

translucent
virginal

thin tongues
of hope
crying
in darkness

Found Poem

Caren Masem

Yesterday I went in search of a poem.
I needed one—in my heart and in my head.
As soon as I opened my eyes I could see
the letters dancing—the *s*'s curving,
the *m*'s and *n*'s with rounded tops.
I lay in bed and listened to vowels singing.
Those sensual sirens—deep *a*'s and *o*'s—
I could not bring them together.
Prepared for hard labor,
I mined my memories,
lighting the way with candles of thought.
The days and nights brightened into years
becoming more and more clear.
Ollie, Ollie, oxen free.
Then I found those verses hiding
in my cluttered attic . . .
All of those letters—consonants and vowels together
lined up in their best order—
my poem came alive.

No Poems

Judith Behar

For weeks, the grass
has been too wet
for mowing:
rain in the night,
clouds every morning,
then the sun burns through,
the air heats up, heavy, humid,
more clouds move in, thunder bounces
off hot pavement, showers pour down.
There have been no poems.

Early morning, damp, cooler,
late summer smells
recall a weekend in the Catskills
when it rained.
Aged eight to fifteen,
the cousins played strip poker in the barn.
Around a damp wooden table,
beneath a dangling light bulb,
they shuffled and dealt the cards,
excited, laughing, clothes coming off—
who knew or made the rules?
Then an explosion of mothers:
"What's going on?"
"Put on your shirt!"
and anger at the oldest:
"What's wrong with you? What were you thinking?"

Not a poem exactly, dim memory
of another time;
then boredom bordered on discovery,
and nakedness and sex
contained the mystery
of what the fuss was for.

Farewell to Poetry

Gail Barger

This poem is done.
It has ceased to exist.
So don't bring me your love stories
or your pain.
Don't tell me about the gold streak
the moon spread across the ocean,
how it was all you could see
and how you wondered what it looked like
from below.
I don't want to hear your pretty words
and especially not your sad ones,
when the fog was so thick
you felt part of it, alone and afraid
and how you ran to get out.

It's over. This poem is done.
From now until what happens,
what you feel, what you see
will exist then and there and be gone.

Poet on Ice

Susan Dean Wessells

One
tentative
syllable
after another
I move:

A skater
with weak ankles,
perched
on narrow blades.

I wobble on words
(while visions
of ice-dancing
glide
through my mind).

I hope
I don't take
an

Ogden
Nashty

fall.

Index of Poets

About the Poets

Catherine Ashley-Nelson, retired from the faculty of North Carolina Agricultural and Technical State University, has been a member of the Writers' Group of the Triad (WGOT) since its inception, circa 1990–91. She was initially in three groups (fiction, non-fiction, and poetry) but currently is only involved with the poetry group. She has participated in creating past anthologies, working with the poetry collection during the first year of WGOT and later editing the mixed-genre collection *Wordworks*.

Gail Barger began writing poetry at a young age as a way of expressing her feelings and observations, a personal method of keeping a journal. After her retirement from North Carolina Agricultural and Technical State University, she began to examine her work with a new eye and started attending poetry workshops. This is her first publication.

A retired lawyer, **Judith Behar** has published poems in *Main Street Rag, Broad River Review, Crucible, Lines from a Near Country, Wordworks,* and other publications. Her poems have won prizes or received honorable mentions in the North Carolina State University poetry contest, the North Carolina Poetry Society contest, *Crucible,* and *Balticon*. She participates in Mystery Writers II and the New Garden Friends Poetry Group.

Lynne Martin Bowman was *Comstock Review's* 2009 Jessie Bryce Niles National Chapbook Contest Winner for her 2010 chapbook, *Water Never Sleeps*. She was *Sonora Review's* Poetry Prize Winner, a 2011 *Crab Orchard Review* Poetry Prize finalist, received honorable mention in the Randall Jarrell Poetry Competition, and was twice an Emily Dickinson Award finalist. Her work has appeared in *Southern Poetry Review, Mississippi Review, International Poetry Review, Sow's Ear Poetry Review, Grasslands' Review,* and *International Icarus*. She lives in Greensboro, North Carolina with her husband and rescued dogs and cat.

Dr. Jane Gibson Brown is the Director of Technical Writing at North Carolina Agricultural and Technical State University. She has published in *Guilford Woman* and in an anthology, *From A Near Country*. She lives in downtown Greensboro with her cat, Fergus.

New to publishing her poetry, **Rhoda Cerny** enjoys the poetry of Emily Bronte, Neruda, Prevert, Baudelaire, Garcia Lorca, Po Chu-i, Patrick Kavanagh, Stevie Smith, and many others. She is working on her first novel.

Diana Engel is in her sixth year as facilitator for the Poetry Writers critique group. Previously a reference and instruction librarian at Guilford College, she has created and led a twelve-week poetry workshop at Penn-Griffin Middle School and taught poetry writing classes at the Greensboro School of Creativity. Her poetry can be found in *The Shagbark Review, Wordworks*, and most recently in *Wild Goose Poetry Review*.

A. C. Hardy is a pharmacist with a passion for writing poetry and plays. His work has appeared in *Kakalak Anthology of Carolina Poets, ByLine Magazine, The Anthology of New England Writers*, and other publications. Mr. Hardy resides in Harrisburg, North Carolina and is also a member of the Charlotte Writers' Club and Dramatists Guild of America.

Muriel Hoff, originally from New York, has lived in North Carolina for many years. In addition to two books of poetry, *Messages Via Muriel* and *The Voice in The Middle of the Night*, she has written *Alphabet Rhymes for Children up to Ninety*.

Julius Howell, a longtime member of the Poetry Writers' group, recently moved to Arizona, where he continues to write.

Nancy Jackson is an active poet who participates in the Poetry Writers group. She resides in Greensboro, North Carolina.

Robin E. Kelly is new to the poetry scene but not new to writing. He is the author of *Aim is the Game in Pool*, a pool and billiards instructional book. Working on this project helped him to rediscover his love of writing, and he plans to write another book on pool. His favorite poet is William Wordsworth, and "I Wandered Lonely as a Cloud" is his favorite poem of all time.

Coventry Kessler, a staff writer and editor at The University of North Carolina at Greensboro, is also a poet and a crank. Unlike Wordsworth ("emotion recollected in tranquility"), Coventry writes "in hot blood" and, sadly for legitimate aspirations, mostly about love. Her poems have appeared in *Iris Magazine*, numerous yellow pads, and emails with a friend she's not embarrassed to show them to. She has fussed at fellow Poetry Writers since 2005 and was delighted to get her grubby little paws on this anthology as a primary editor.

Lois Losyk is a new poet who is thrilled to have found her creativity late in life. "A Conversation With Those Taken," her first published poem, was selected for the September 11, 2011 online edition of the Greensboro *News & Record*. She finds that being immersed in the art of writing poetry is a spiritual and joyful experience.

Rosalyn Marhatta lives in her own world to write poetry and pops out to perform at Tate Street Coffee House and the Greensboro Public Library. She decided to be a poet after her sister insisted her stories were really poems. She's published in *Dead Mule, Referential Magazine, Poems2Day, Diamond Diva Magazine, Eclectic Flash* and *Vox Poetica*. For her poem "Ocean Flight," first published in *Vox Poetica*, she has been nominated for a Pushcart Prize.

Caren Masem has written and taught poetry for many years at both university and high school levels, as well as in writing workshops. She earned an MA in English at Iowa State. Her poems appear in several anthologies, including *In the Yard* and *Mountain High*, published by Old Mountain Press, and in *Appalachian Writers Guild Anthology MMVII, Wild Goose Poetry Review*, and *Dead Mule*. She was a finalist in the South Carolina Poetry Foundation Contest and was published in *The State* newspaper in Columbia.

Stephanie McManus is a working poet living with her husband and pets in Greensboro, North Carolina. She graduated from the University of Florida in psychology and currently works in county mental health. Her poetry can be found online at www.stephaniesattic.wordpress.com. Stephanie has been noted in the blogosphere by Alaskan poet D.C. McKenzie as "fearless and prolific... a multi-faceted writer, by turns insightful and whimsical, perceptive and daring."

Barbara Baillet Moran is a former professional storyteller whose poems often tell stories. A member of New Garden Friends Poetry Group, her poetry was included in *Lines From Another Country* and *A Turn in Time*. Her poem, "Filling Spaces," written on September 11, 2001, was part of a multi-media exhibit in a New York City gallery throughout October and November, 2001. Stanzas of the same poem were engraved into the large steel sculpture by Jim Gallucci that paid tribute to those who perished in the catastrophe of 9/11.

Fran Ostasiewski serves as treasurer of the WGOT and enjoys organizing Poetry, Jazz & Java events. While he has written other types of poetry, he is partial to haiku, which have appeared in *Walking the Same Path, Rose Haiku for Flower Lovers and Gardeners, Frogpond*, and *White Lies*.

Walt Pilcher wrote parody radio commercials at age eleven, foreshadowing a career in consumer products marketing. He moonlighted as a fiction and song writer, publishing a story in the first issue of *Galileo* magazine and satire in *The Worm Runner's Digest*. He was a contributing editor of *In-Store Marketing* by Michael Wahl and an editor and first-reader of *More than We Can Imagine* by Rev. Dick Robinson. He is also a member of the Greensboro Playwrights' Forum and NC Writers' Network and an alumnus of writing classes at the Greensboro School of Creativity and The University of North Carolina at Greensboro.

Since earning her MFA in Creative Writing from The University of North Carolina at Greensboro, **Sandra Redding** has published three books: *Greensboro: Portrait of Progress* (Community Communications); *Winston-Salem: Bright Star of the Future* (Community Communications); and a memoir, *Greensboro & Me: Dancing through the Decade* (Alabaster Press). She has over twenty-five short stories, more than fifty poems, and hundreds of book reviews and feature articles in print. Currently she writes a column for the Greensboro *News & Record* and leads memoir workshops for Shepherd's Center and WGOT.

Poet **Jean Rodenbough,** author of five books, is a retired Presbyterian minister. Her next book includes stories of animals who experience tragic conditions until taken in by those whose love and care change their lives. Poems add commentary.

Anya Russian is a poet and dance artist from Greensboro. Her poetry grapples with the limitations of understanding the wavering boundaries between people and their environment, cultures, and selves. In 2010 she received the Poet Laureate Award from the North Carolina Poetry Society. Her poetry has been published in *Pinesong*, included in the Nazim Hikmet Poetry Festival (2010), and most recently appears in the *International Poetry Review*. Her first chapbook of poetry is forthcoming from Unicorn Press in 2012.

Cynthia Strauff Schaub is a retired executive who, after years of nurturing career and left brain, has given her right brain full authority over her. She recently was awarded first prize for her poem, "Emily Anderson," at the Ashe County Literary Festival. She spends her days writing and staring out at the trees.

Janice Sullivan, past president of the WGOT, is presently co-facilitator of the Tuesday afternoon poetry critique group. She has been published in *A Turn in Time, International Icarus, Pembroke Magazine,*